The Dead Bird

Text copyright 1938 by Margaret Wise Brown

Text copyright renewed 1965 by Roberta Brown Rauch

Illustrations copyright © 2016 by Christian Robinson

All rights reserved. Printed in the United States of America.

No part of this book may be used or reproduced in

any manner whatsoever without written permission

except in the case of brief quotations embodied in

critical articles and reviews. For information address

HarperCollins Children's Books,

a division of HarperCollins Publishers,

195 Broadway, New York, NY 10007.

www.harpercollinschildrens.com

ISBN 978-0-06-028931-7

The artist used traditional media and Photoshop

to create the illustrations for this book.

Typography by Martha Rago

16 17 18 19 PC 10 9 8 7 6 5 4 3 2

❖

Newly Illustrated Edition, 2016

Originally published in 1938 by

Addison-Wesley Publishing Company

THE DEAD BIRD

STORY BY
MARGARET WISE BROWN

PICTURES BY
CHRISTIAN ROBINSON

HARPER
An Imprint of HarperCollinsPublishers

The bird was dead when the children found it.

But it had not been dead for long—it was still warm and its eyes were closed.

The children felt with their fingers for the quick beat of the bird's heart in its breast.

But there was no heart beating.
That was how they knew it was dead.

And even as they held it, it began to get cold, and the limp bird body grew stiff, so they couldn't bend its legs and the head didn't flop when they moved it.

That was the way animals got when
they had been dead for some time—
cold dead and stone still with no heart
beating.

The children were very sorry the bird was dead
and could never fly again. But they were glad
they had found it, because now they could dig

a grave in the woods and bury it. They could have
a funeral and sing to it the way grown-up people did
when someone died.

So they took it out in the woods.

And they dug a hole in the ground.

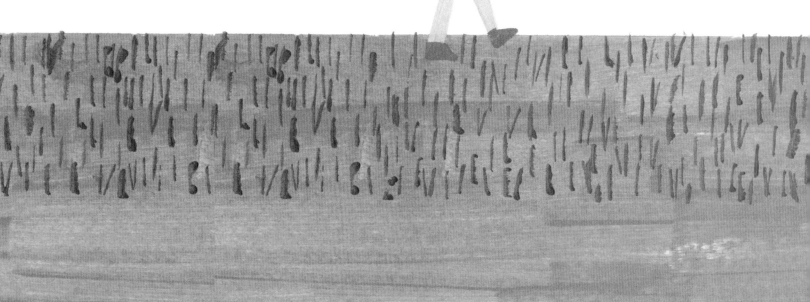

They put warm sweet-ferns in the bottom of the grave.
And they wrapped the bird up in grapevine leaves
and put it in the ground.

Then they put more ferns on top of it, and little
white violets, and yellow star flowers.

Then they sang a song to it:

Oh bird you're dead
You'll never fly again
Way up high
With other birds in the sky
We sing to you
Because you're dead
Feather bird
And we buried you
In the ground
With ferns and flowers
Because you will never fly
Again in the sky
Way up high
Little dead bird.

Then they cried because their singing was so beautiful and the ferns smelled so sweetly and the bird was dead.

They put dirt over the bird as they sang, and then they put more ferns and flowers and a gray stone on top of the dirt.

On the stone they wrote:

Around the stone they planted white violet plants, and wild geraniums, only the geraniums faded.

And every day, until they forgot, they went
and sang to their little dead bird and put fresh
flowers on his grave.